A WORLD WITHOUT RAIN

BY
WILLIAM ANTHONY

BookLife PUBLISHING

©2021
BookLife Publishing Ltd.
King's Lynn
Norfolk PE30 4LS

A catalogue record for this book is available from the British Library.

ISBN: 978-1-83927-138-0

Written by:
William Anthony

Edited by:
Robin Twiddy

Designed by:
Drue Rintoul

IMAGE CREDITS

4&5 – wavebreakmedia, ND700. 6&7 – Arisa_J, NazArt, HelloRF Zcool, DiA99. 8&9 – Jaromir Chalabala, Fabien Monteil. 10&11 – 3355m. 12&13 – Thongden Studio, ER_09, Kristina Kokhanova, kwest, leolintang, Galyna Andrushko. 14&15 – Erin Donalson, Gorodenkoff. 16&17 – CGN089, DenisMArt. 18&19 – aslysun, Alessandro Cristiano. 20&21 – vchal, ADragan. 22&23 – Riccardo Mayer, hagit berkovich. All images courtesy of Shutterstock.com. With thanks to Getty Images, Thinkstock Photo and iStockphoto.

CONTENTS

Words that look like this can be found in the glossary on page 24.

WHAT COULD YOU LIVE WITHOUT?

Some people give things up that are bad for them. What could you give up? Reading books? No chance – books are good for you!

Books are way too much fun to give up!

There are worse things to lose than books. What if it never rained again and we ran out of water? That's a scary thought!

GO ON, BE BRAVE. TURN THE PAGE AND SEE WHAT A WORLD WITHOUT RAIN COULD LOOK LIKE...

Mum, There's a Bit of a Problem...

Mum

What have you done now? 😡

Nothing! There's an issue with our river boat trip.

TELL ME WHAT YOU'VE DONE, GRAHAM.

Mum, I haven't done anything!

Well what is it then?

The river... It's kind of gone.

Rain is part of the water cycle. The Sun heats up water until it evaporates. It cools and forms clouds. After time, those clouds will rain. The rain finds its way back into oceans through rivers. This means that if it never rained again, rivers would dry up!

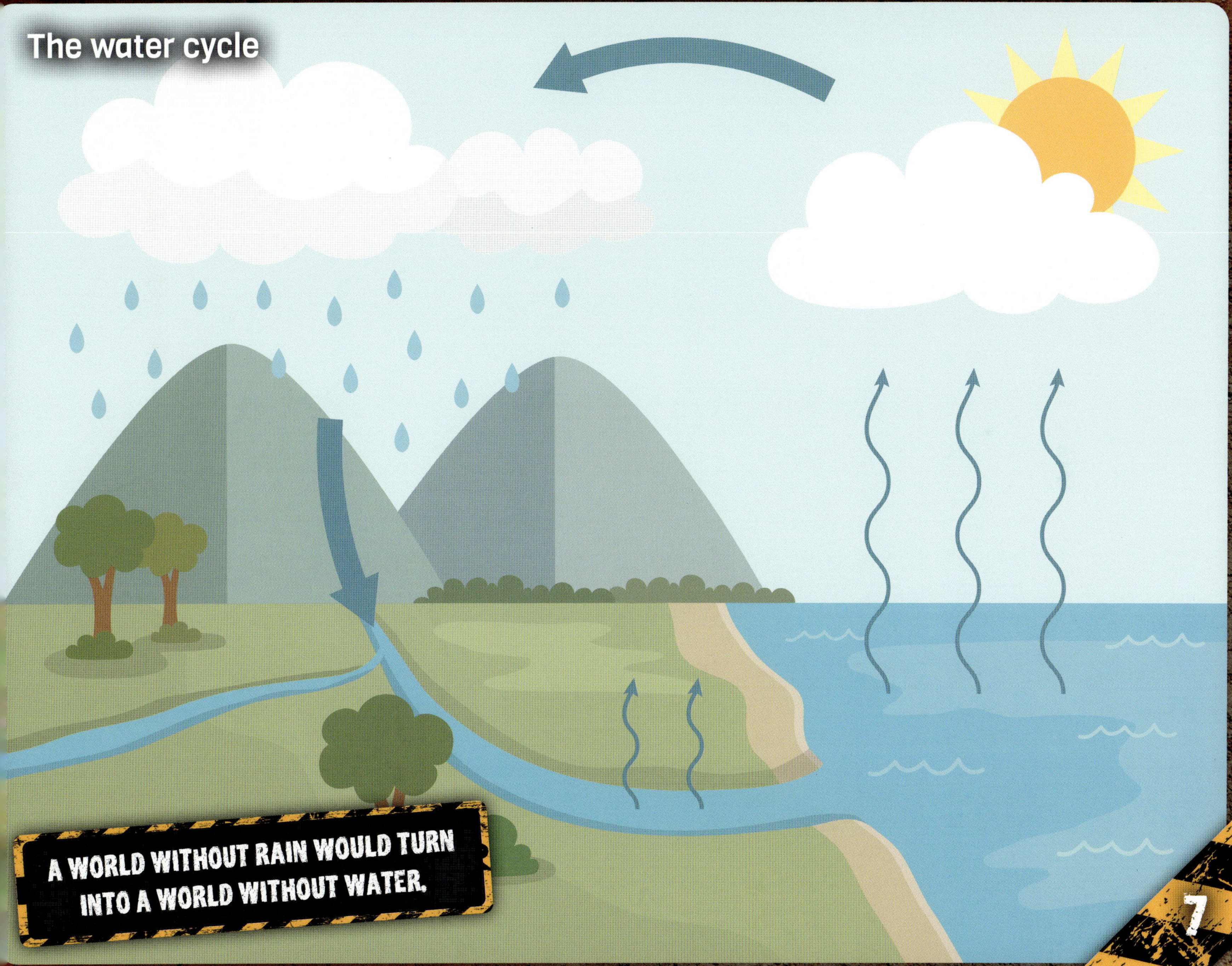

A WORLD WITHOUT RAIN WOULD TURN INTO A WORLD WITHOUT WATER.

DEPARTURES
TIME DESTINATION FLIGHT GATE REMARKS
12:28 NEW YORK BA 903 31 CANCELLED
12:46 SYDNEY QF5723 27 CANCELLED
13:08 TORONTO AC5984 22 CANCELLED
13:21 TOKYO JL 608 41 DELAYED
13:37 HONG KONG CX5471 29 CANCELLED
13:48 MADRID IB3941 30 DELAYED
14:19 BERLIN LH5021 28 CANCELLED
14:35 LONDON AA 997 11 CANCELLED
14:54 PARIS AF5870 23 DELAYED
15:10 ROME AZ5324 43 CANCELLED

Clouds are made from air and tiny drops of water. If it never rained again, those drops of water wouldn't have anywhere to go. This could leave us with a sky full of thick clouds, which might make things such as flying aeroplanes very difficult!

So many clouds would make it difficult for pilots to see.

Gardening
Weekly
18th May 2024
No Rain?
No Problem (Yet)!
Fill your garden with the only plants on Earth – get your cacti before they die!
Are YOU a Cactus? Take our test on page 12!
Plants from the Past: Our top 10 plants before the rain stopped
How to Avoid Injury When Decorating Your Cactus for Christmas
13 Ways You Shouldn't Sit on Your Cactus

Plants need water to live. Without any rain, plants would struggle to survive. Some plants, such as cacti, would be able to live for a few years without rain, but after that, all plants would be dead.

CACTI CAN STORE LOTS OF WATER, SO THEY WOULD LIVE UNTIL THEIR STORES RAN OUT.

DREARYDAY | Search results for: novelty frogs

http://www.drearydaygetaways.com

DREARYDAY GETAWAYS

Home

About

Holidays

Contact

Get away with DrearyDay this summer!

Book now!

Italy

Experience the wonderful cities and perfectly dry land that Italy has to offer.

Japan

Catch some of the summer cloud in stunning, waterless Japan.

Mexico

Get away from the cities and explore the Mexican wasteland.

After around one year without rain, most of the Earth would have desert-like conditions. This means there would be very little water left in lakes and rivers, and the land would become completely dry.

I Won't Lie To You – Everything's on Fire

The clouds don't rain anymore, London's burning again and old forests are in flames. We don't even have enough water left to put it all out. Many people's pants are actually on fire.

As the land and plants continue to dry out, wildfires would become a big risk. Dried-out plants are the perfect fuel for wildfires. Wildfires can spark during very dry weather.

With hardly any water left, it would be difficult to put out wildfires.

H2GO MARKETPLACE

Search results for: novelty pogs

http://www.h2omkt.com

H_2GO

Bottle of Water

Only 855 left!

£3,600,000

- Be the talk of the town and stay topped up on water!
- Stay healthy when others can't!
- Avoid getting ill and survive a little longer!

Add to Basket

Expected Delivery: 3–5 days

Around two-thirds of your body is made of water, and you need it to live. With water almost completely gone, people would begin to get very dehydrated. Being dehydrated can make you very ill.

The last bottles of water could become very expensive.

A ◆nice◆ big ~~bowl~~ bottle of Delicious ~~News~~ Water!

I'm so thirsty.

DOCTORS IN CATCH TWENTY-POO

As the last water dries up, waiting times to see doctors rise to over FOUR days.

Doctors have limited their help to wee draining and poo removal only, as waiting times have risen higher than ever before.

Water, water nowhere, and not a drop to drink.

Water levels have reached critical lows this last week, with the final few hundred ...les going on sale for

Without any water left to drink, we would have trouble going to the toilet. Water helps us to get rid of waste from our bodies. Without it, doctors could have to help remove our wee and poo for us!

When the water dries up after the rain stops, it will not be a pretty picture.

SMELL IT
BANG
For when it all gets too much...
SMELL IT
BANG

Water is important for flushing away toilet waste. Water takes our waste into sewers on its way to be cleaned before being sent out to sea. If all the water finally dried up, our waste couldn't be washed away and things would get very smelly!

PEOPLE COULD TURN TO AIR FRESHENERS TO COVER UP THE SMELL.

IT STARTS WITH US

That was terrifying, wasn't it? Relax, rain isn't going to suddenly stop falling and all the water isn't going to just dry up. However, lots of people in our world do not have access to much water at all.

A world without rain led to a world without water and we saw how terrible that would be. You can help people get access to water by supporting a charity such as WaterAid. We must care for everyone so that nobody lives without water.

GLOSSARY

conditions the state of the environment, such as the temperature, rainfall and food available

dehydrated to not have drunk enough water for the body to work properly

evaporates turns from a liquid, like water, into a gas or vapour, usually through heat

fuel something that can be used to make energy

sewers pipes that are usually underground, used to carry off water and sewage

two-thirds two of three equal parts of something

waste the things that the human body gets rid of, such as wee and poo

wildfires fires, usually in natural places, that burn quickly and are difficult to control

INDEX